ONCE TO DIE.

BY RON ABRAHAM

Published by New Generation Publishing in 2013

Copyright © Ron Abraham 2013

First Edition

www.newgeneration-publishing.com

New Generation Publishing

INTRODUCTION

The meaning and purpose of life on earth have challenged the minds of men for centuries.

Why are we born?

How should we live?

Why do we live the way we do?

Is it the best way?

What is the use of having life?

What is important and what is not?

Is there life when life on earth ends?

Question, questions and more questions and as reggae artist Jimmy Cliff sings, "there are more questions than answers."

Concrete answers to these questions are few, but one truth that all men believe is

"it is given to men once to die."

Throughout this book **my meaning for the word 'man' is men and women,** i.e. humanity.

This book strives to find answers and gives a concept that tries to explain the meaning of life, looking through events on earth and may possibly impact ideas and concepts embedded in our minds.

I believe in Jesus Christ and have proven, in my lifetime, that Holy Scripture can be relied on as truth so I have made use sparingly of bible quotes, for some of my references and I believe that what was stated many years ago by Sir Frederick Kenyon, former Director of the British Museum, when he wrote, "both the authenticity and the general integrity of the books of the New Testament may be regarded as established." I therefore agree with such an illustrious person and therefore have no difficulty in assuming credibility.

Pilate the Roman procurator asked of Jesus, "what is truth?" indeed a very meaningful question as some people regard anything coming from their mouth as truth and that from anyone else's as lies.

I believe that truth comes from Jesus Christ who is spiritually known as the way, the truth and even life itself.

Sometimes one truly believes what one is saying is true, then his knowledge and experience increases and he understands, then, that what he believed on previously was not true. This has happened to me and I am sure it has happened to you and the same applies to things that have been inculcated into our brains as youths; we often discover later that they were never true in the present life circumstances that we are often faced with.

CHAPTER 1
BIRTH

It is commonly held by scholars that life begins when someone takes his or her first unaided breath.

Ideas are born at the moment of conception.

Plants, as soon as they sprout.

Animals, as soon as they come out of their mothers and take their first unaided breath.

Human beings therefore are born when they take their first unaided breath. That being so, could a person be born more than once? Generally one would say no, however, the birth of an event in a person's life could have so much impact as to change the person irreversibly for the rest of their life. This then could be termed as receiving new life or born again or a "eureka" moment, after Galileo's expression which was born when he discovered the answer to a problem he was faced with that was troubling him for some time.

Birth of a human being could be as a result of man and woman coming together or Spirit and woman resulting in a birth. This birth commences a process called life where the person born is trained to be able to survive in their environment or world later along the path of life.

This life will continue until the time of end or death; in other words, we start our journey towards death with life being termed as the interval between birth and death.

In the early part of life one has to provide the brain with information and experiences (knowledge) which would make one better equipped for having a "good life" later.

Life therefore could be expressed as the interval from adolescence to death which could be measured in economic terms as from 15 to 65, or 50 years, although some people from planning or circumstance extend this time.

How is a good life different to a "bad life"? What are the criteria to judge the difference? Is life lived on earth and followed by a judgement at the end? If so, by whom?

Could the life lived itself impose its own judgement? For example, could not a life lived eating in excess cause one to become obese and would not the resulting health problems be classed as the judgment imposed from the lifestyle choice?

Concepts of "a good life" are usually handed down from generation to generation and vary considerably from country to country and sometimes even within the same country.

It is commonly held that each generation tries to remove the hardships and difficulties that they faced in their own life from that of their children's, thus attempting to make their children's lives better than their own.

While this concept is good, could not the possibility exist that the circumstances of their own lives would have been different to that of their children causing them to require new skills for survival which their parents were unable to give, resulting in the children having new difficulties not faced by their ancestors and so the cycle of different hardships continue?Later on in this book we will deal with a "good life" in an attempt to find common ground for an acceptable definition.

CHAPTER TWO
FORMATION

This period of time is the wonderful opportunity given to the parents and extended families to "shape" the baby with basic social skills, manners, morals and generally with well-rounded abilities which will prepare this new person for whatever comes later on in life.

Sadly, it does not always work so, as often people pass on their hurts, biases and fears which often have the opposite effect.

EARLY DAYS.
Basic skills like potty training enable the little one to recognise when they need to go to toilet, then they are helped to crawl and walk while their food is mixed until they can cope with solid foods. One could say that this is obvious but if such basic skills are not done properly this baby could grow up to have antisocial habits and behaviour that could be most embarrassing and difficult to break later. Hence the saying "well-fed but badly bred" could apply.

HOME.

The place called 'home' is generally where Mum and Dad take control for the child's formative years. The child listens to and observes everything that is said and done and as he grows in knowledge he even observes the contradictions when things said do not match the things done.

Simple things are picked up like mum or dad's fear of all dogs or types of dogs. That is learned so when the child sees dogs of the type the child is afraid and wants to take defensive action.

The child also picks up likes and dislikes of certain people from the home so as soon as he sees the type discussed in the home he is on guard and could even hate those persons for no reason.

He picks similarly likes and dislikes for certain types of music, he can become affectionate or not, he can become caring or not, sensitive to needs around him or selfish all from what he sees and hears so his likes and dislikes are learnt from his home environment.

At this same time, his dad or mum become his mentors with the end result that he is "formed" to be who he is "so much like his dad or mum."

SCHOOL.

The great day arrives when he goes to school and then he is exposed to another mentor, "teacher," and if teacher says something which contradicts what his first mentors at home have said, we get the all-familiar expression, "but Mummy or Daddy, teacher said…"

At the same time his friend or friends also start to influence him and he now is exposed to "peer pressure."

During this period continuing up to high school the child is being bombarded with influences at home and at school and the great teacher, "television" plays a large part in his formation with the demand that they all make for his time and attention.

Fortunately he spends a large part of his time at home enabling his parents, by and large, the greatest share of his formative years which would still put in the parents' hand the ability to do the most good in instilling sound morals and discipline, and if this fails to happen the end result could easily be mal-formation in one or several areas.

These factors, at a time when the child has not as yet formed his "own" opinions, opens the door for various outcomes when he eventually enters the area of focus of this book, which is called life.

There could be good results depending on how astute the parents are to observe inclinations and strengths, encouraging the good ones and discouraging the bad ones.

Imagine the possibility when a person, as yet not properly formed themselves, has children of his or her own; one can well imagine the possible outcome later in life and the difficulties that could be faced by that adult.

This period called formation would play a major part in enabling a person to have his share of a good life later, although there are examples of some persons who became successful despite the difficulties.

CHAPTER THREE
CONCEPTS OF LIFE

When one is a minor, i.e. up to age 18 years, basic education becomes a key activity spurred on by ideas handed down by one's parents and elder relatives who generally endeavour to see that related minors are helped to be able to do equal or better than themselves in their later walk called life.

Concepts are put into the minor's brain such as "study hard so one day you can be a lawyer, doctor, scientist, engineer, dentist, etc."

All pictures conjured by the parents, though very good in their minds, may finish up having no real relevance to the life of the new person in time to come.

Let us take an example: a doctor studies hard and qualifies. He now works long hours and may even be on call when he is off duty and so he has very little time for fun and social interaction for which he then takes home about £5000 a month.

A man, on the other hand, working at a stall on the market sells about 300 bowls of fruit a day at £1 for 5 days a week, he grosses £6000 a month.

Say after expenses he nets £3000. He has every weekend off, he finishes work at 6:00 daily, goes out with his family to the movies etc. Is the doctor's life better than the fruit man? (The example is used here only to open minds and not to build up one against the other or to discriminate in any way.)

Maybe the thought could be introduced here that one should choose what they love doing as a career and then he is more likely to accept what that choice demands of him.

These former ideas of a good life are well inculcated into the minor's brain until he or she becomes self-motivated in their studying and working to achieve the "good life."

Learning takes so much of their energies and time that examination of the concepts handed down are rarely done, with the outcome that many adhere to a concept of a "good life" that is actually foreign to them.

Ideas like buying a nice house in a well sought after area, owning a good brand of car, being able to afford membership to top clubs, being able to afford to eat at top expensive restaurants, being able to afford holidays to exotic places, wearing nice clothes, being seen with top people, having pretty boyfriends or girlfriends are all collectively seen as the "dolce vita," a good life.

There are many examples of people who have achieved "the good life" portrayed in the media such as footballers, models, actresses, heiresses, wives and girlfriends of sportspeople called " WAGS"

Others who earn millions of dollars in bonuses, like city bankers, are seen as role models and sometimes even envied but there have been several cases in the press of such men killing themselves when bonuses drop from ten million, let's say to two million. Consider how many people would be happy for even a thousand dollars in bonus.

With such pictures in mind, minors are encouraged to study hard in order to position themselves to acquire their portion of "the good life."

While carrying such a motivational force in mind, anything else is seen as a failure and cannot be tolerated, giving vent to idioms such as "if at first you don't succeed try, try, try again;" thus, modern man is programmed to seek success at any price so they can enjoy " the good life."

IS IT WRONG TO ACHIEVE SUCH THINGS? CERTAINLY NOT, BUT IT IS NOT THE COMPLETE PICTURE.

HOW DOES ONE BECOME SUCCESSFUL?

The word 'successful' is understood as being when someone is good at something or some things as attested to by peers or others.

Or in business when one provides a profitable service or product that is in demand.

Or when one has a unique talent that others will pay handsomely for.

This entails constant dedicated focus on the something or activity that is in demand requiring of the provider many hours and in some instances years of disciplined hard work even to the point and beyond of self- sacrifice.

In provision of services it would entail consistent quality and reliability in that provision, meaning regardless of the day, hour or weather the service is made to be available. A typical example is a 24/7 corner shop.

These activities often require sacrifice of the self to achieve success which could easily bring the idiom 'all work and no play makes Jack a dull boy,' hence the conflict that acquisition of success could easily restrict enjoyment of that success.

If, on the other hand, the success is enjoyed abundantly that would almost certainly affect the success itself, with it resulting in reduction of success, so balance is often called for between the striving after and enjoyment of success.

Take a champion boxer who wins a belt. To increase his worth or success he has to defend his belt, for there are always others waiting to take it from him. If after winning the belt he takes a few weeks off to enjoy his success, his sharpness decreases, he becomes sluggish and could lose his belt and success so he becomes a slave to his success to maintain it.Hence the "good life" could easily enslave one in order to continue to be in a position to maintain it. This brings to mind that which is written in the book of Ecclasiates1"Vanities of Vanities," making the good life without happiness a "chase after wind."

These examples are all in the physical domain; however, there is another level of success in the spiritual realm while on earth, such as when someone has surrendered his life to Jesus Christ (termed being born again) and is living in the knowledge of what is expected of him and is walking blamelessly in that path. That indeed in my opinion is the ultimate success even if that person is not making much money, although he may also be successful in the physical domain.

ACCUMULATION OF WEALTH.

Some people, very few, are born into wealth and it is said that those who inherit it do not often have a sense of appreciation for the privilege, although there are exceptions.

When one becomes successful wealth usually follows. Then 1 million worth gives way to ten million and eventually billions. This wealth is confined to this life and when the time comes to depart it is all left behind.

Wouldn't it be nice, as the pharoahs of Egypt dreamed, to carry wealth with one into the next life whatever it may be?

Is it possible to do so?

I say yes, it is possible. However, physical wealth has to be converted to non-physical currency which could be accumulated in the next world while being here on earth.

It starts with preparing oneself, while on earth, for reception of a heavenly disposition.

This calls for one to be born again, preparing oneself for eternal life when life on Earth ends by a simple prayer in faith: "Lord Jesus I want to be born again, I surrender my life to you and accept that you died on the cross for me, please come into my life today." Once that is done the person is ready to do the conversion of currency.

The currency here on Earth is money, thus the value of everything is converted to dollars as a measurement, i.e. gold is measured as so many dollars per ounce.

The currency of the next world beyond death is good works or bad works.

The word of God as stated in[and?] the Bible makes it clear about the conversion of earthly wealth:

Matthew 6:19-21

"Do not lay up for yourselves treasures on earth, where moth and rust destroy and where thieves break in and steal, but lay up for yourselves treasures in heaven, where neither moth nor rust destroys and where thieves do not break in and steal. For where your treasure is, there your heart will be also."

Luke 12:33-34

"Sell what you have and give alms, get purses for yourselves that do not wear out, a never-failing treasure with the Lord which no thief comes near nor any moth destroys. Wherever your treasure lies, there your heart will be."

In other words as worldly treasure abounds, one should use it to do the things which convert it such as feeding the poor, clothing the naked, housing the homeless among other good deeds for those less fortunate.

This has a two-dimensional reward system attached to it:

1) Being born again causes this conversion of treasure to act like some kind of insurance which could ensure continuation of wealth here on earth, if handled wisely.

2) Conversion allows treasures in heavenly currency to be built up in the other world where no one can steal or hack it as it waits for the eventual departure of the person from this world with no freight charges, no tax or duty or even storage charges.

Another question comes to mind: does acquisition of a "good life" cause happiness to the one enjoying it? Are they always happy or happy at all?

To find the answer we have to look at history, in the public domain records to see that a search would reveal there have been many examples of achievers of the good life in various walks of life who had it but did not find happiness.

ACTORS/ ACTRESSES

Gwili Andre (1959), distinguished Danish actress, killed herself by self-immolation despite her success and fame.

Gwili Andre
Date of Birth
4 February 1908, Copenhagen, Denmark

Date of Death
5 February 1959, Venice, California, USA (suicide)

Birth Name
Gurli Andresen

Height
5' 6" (1.68 m)

Mini Biography
Danish-born Gwili Andre was a blonde beauty who had the talent and the looks necessary for the big time, but somehow just couldn't put everything together and was mired in B pictures (e.g., Secrets of the French Police (1932), Roar of the Dragon (1932)) for most of her career. After retiring from the screen, she died in an apartment fire in 1959.

IMDb   Mini   Biography   By:
frankfob2@yahoo.com

Trivia

Her death in 1959 was a bizarre suicide after years of alcoholism and failed attempts to revive her stalled career. Alone in her Venice, California apartment she gathered together reams of publicity stills and promotional material from her early career and set it alight, allowing herself also to be consumed by the flames. She died later of her injuries.

Max Linder

Max Linder (1925), French film and stage actor double-suicided with his wife by Verona by morphine injections and cut wrists despite his success and fame.

From Wikipedia, the free encyclopedia

Born	Gabriel-Maximilien Leuvielle December 16, 1883 Cavernes, Saint-Loubès, Gironde, France
Died	October 31, 1925 (aged 41) Paris, France
Occupation	Actor, film director, screenwriter, film producer, comedian
Years active	1899–1925
Spouse(s)	Heléne "Jean" Peters (1923-1925) (one daughter)

Gabriel-Maximilien Leuvielle
(16 December 1883 – 31 October 1925), better known by the stage name **Max Linder** (French: [lin.dɛʁ]), was a French actor, director, screenwriter, producer and comedian of the silent film era. His onscreen persona "Max" was one of the first recognizable recurring characters in film.

Born in Cavernes, France to Catholic parents, Linder grew up with a passion for the theatre and enrolled in the Bordeaux Conservatorie in 1899. He soon received awards for his performances and continued to pursue a career in the legitimate theatre. He became a contract player with the Bordeaux Théâtre des Arts from 1901 to 1904, performing in plays by <u>Molière</u>, <u>Pierre Corneille</u> and <u>Alfred de Musset</u>.

In the early 1900s, Linder appeared in short comedy films for Pathé, usually in supporting roles. His first major film role was in the Georges Méliès-like fantasy film *The Legend of Punching*. During the following years, Linder made more than one hundred short films portraying "Max," a wealthy and dapper man-about-town frequently in hot water because of his penchant for beautiful women and the good life. Starting with *The Skater's Debut* in 1907, the character became one of the first identifiable motion-picture characters who appeared in successive situation comedies. In 1911, Linder began co-directing his own films (with René LePrince) as well as writing the scripts.

During the First World War, Linder worked as a dispatch driver and entertainer. It was during this time he suffered his first outbreak of chronic depression. In 1918, Linder moved to the United States, where he became a major star and formed his own production company in 1921. After a brief move back to France, he returned to the United States and made *Seven Years Bad Luck* and *Be My Wife* but neither were able to find many American fans. Other films followed, including *The Three Must-Get-Theres* and *Au Secours!* which became a success with English critics. However, the later films proved unpopular with American audiences and as a result, Linder became depressed. He made his last film *The King of the Circus* in 1925, but his illness worsened. In 1925, he committed suicide along with his wife of two years, Heléne "Jean" Peters.

SINGERS
Kurt Cobain (1994), accomplished American rock singer, killed himself with a gun [or died by self-inflicted gunshot wound].

Death of Kurt Cobain
From Wikipedia, the free encyclopedia

171 Lake Washington Blvd East Seattle, Washington, the site of Cobain's death.

Kurt Cobain, the lead singer of the American grunge band Nirvana, was found dead at his home located at 171 Lake Washington Boulevard in Seattle, Washington, United States on April 8, 1994, having committed suicide three days prior on April 5. The Seattle Police Department incident report states that Cobain was found with a shotgun across his body, had a visible head wound and there was a suicide note discovered nearby. The King County Medical Examiner noted that there were puncture wounds on the inside of both the right and left elbow. Prior to his death, Cobain had checked out of a drug rehabilitation facility and been reported suicidal by his wife Courtney Love.

Despite the official ruling of suicide, several theories have arisen offering alternate explanations for Cobain's death. Tom Grant, a private investigator hired by Cobain's wife, Courtney Love, to find Cobain after his departure from rehab, put forth his belief that Cobain was murdered. Grant's theory has since been analyzed and questioned by television shows, films and books. Authors and filmmakers have also attempted to explain what might have happened during Cobain's final days, and what might have led him to commit suicide.

HEIRS/HEIRESSES

Alice de Janze (1941), American heiress, attempted suicide with a firearm.

Poor Little Rich Girl: Alice de Janze

On March 25, 1927 a well-dressed couple boarded a train at the Gare du Nord. A shot was heard, followed immediately by another. When the conductor opened the door to the compartment, the woman gasped, "I did it," before collapsing. The woman who pulled the trigger was an twenty-seven year old American heiress named Alice de Janzé, married to a French count. The victim was her lover, 32 year old Raymund de Trafford, the son of an English baronet.

WRITERS
Ernest Hemingway (1961), famous American writer and journalist killed himself with gunshot wound to the head.

Synopsis
Born on July 21, 1899, in Cicero (now in Oak Park), Illinois, Ernest Hemingway served in World War I and worked in journalism before publishing his story collection *In Our Time*. He was renowned for novels like *The Sun Also Rises*, *A Farewell to Arms*, *For Whom the Bell Tolls*, and *The Old Man and the Sea*, which won the 1953 Pulitzer. In 1954, Hemingway won the Nobel Prize. He committed suicide on July 2, 1961, in Ketchum, Idaho.

We sympathise with friends and families on their recorded losses but use these references only to show that "the good life" may not in itself induce happiness, peace of mind, joy, satisfaction and balance with the rest of humanity and nature.

If "the good life" fails to achieve happiness, to the point that people enjoying it can choose to end their life then what is missing?

What makes for happiness?

CHAPTER FOUR
HAPPINESS

Happiness is also a topic that has engaged men's minds for centuries.

"I want to be happy" is heard time and time again, but what is happiness?

Can one get hold of this happiness and what does it do, does it cause one to be smiling and singing at all times?

We have seen in the previous chapter that achieving the good life in many walks of life does not sustain happiness. The very thing that has motivated us from early life itself is lacking and could leave the achiever miserable even with all the perks being enjoyed.

In the Metro newspaper of August 18th 2010, it reports under the headline "Millionaire raffles off his luxury villa," that Karl Rabeder a 48 year old (at that time) stated, " I thought the more money I had, the happier I would become, but it was not the case." He was giving away his £3,000,000 wealth and raffling his £1.4 Million villa with £1 tickets while he himself was moving into a bedsit in Innsbruch (Austria)

PARIS: An Austrian tycoon is giving away every penny of his £3 million ($5.3 million) fortune, having realised that his riches made him unhappy.

Karl Rabeder, 47, a businessman from Telfs, near Innsbruck, is selling his villa with lake, sauna and spectacular mountain views over the Alps, valued at £1.4 million.

Also for sale is his old stone farmhouse in Provence, on the market for £613,000. Already gone is his collection of six gliders valued at £350,000.

Mr Rabeder has also sold the interior furnishings and accessories business-- from vases to artificial flowers-- that made his fortune.

"My idea is to have nothing left. Absolutely nothing. Money is counter-productive-- it prevents happiness."

He will move out of his Alpine retreat into a small wooden hut in the mountains or a simple bedsit in Innsbruck, surviving on £800 a month while the proceeds go to a charity he set up in Latin America. He will draw no salary from it.

"For a long time I believed that more wealth and luxury automatically meant more happiness. I come from a very poor family where the rules were to work more to achieve more material things, and I applied this for many years."

But over time a conflicting feeling developed. "More and more I heard the words, 'Stop what you are doing now-- all this luxury and consumerism-- and start your real life.' I had the feeling I was working as a slave for things that I did not wish for or need."

For many years, he said, he was not brave enough to give up his comforts. The tipping point came during a three-week holiday with his wife in Hawaii.

"It was the biggest shock in my life when I realised how horrible, soulless and without feeling the five-star lifestyle is.

"In those three weeks we spent all the money you could possibly spend. But in all that time we had the feeling we hadn't met a single real person - that we were all just actors. The staff played the role of being friendly and the guests played the role of being important, and nobody was real."

Mr Rabeder decided to raffle his Alpine home, selling 21,999 tickets at £87 each. The Provence house, in the village of Cruis, is on sale at the local estate agent.

All the money will go into his microcredit charity, which offers small loans and advice to self-employed people in El Salvador, Honduras, Bolivia, Peru, Argentina and Chile.

Since deciding to sell up, Mr Rabeder said he had felt "free, the opposite of heavy". But he did not judge those who chose to keep their wealth. "I do not have the right to give any other person advice. I was just listening to the voice of my heart and soul."

Telegraph, London

Money and wealth appears not to guarantee happiness, so what is happiness and how is it to be achieved?

In the metro of 8th JULY 2010 the headline "Jolie: I cut myself for the thrills," reported Angelina Jolie as saying, "I used to cut myself or jump out of airplanes, trying to find something new to push up against because sometimes everything else felt too easy," adding, "I was searching for something deeper, something more. I tried everything. I always felt caged, closed in, like

I was punching at things that weren't there. I always had too much energy for the room I was in. I went through a period when I felt my film characters were having more fun than I was."

This leads us back to the question what is happiness, and how is it to be achieved.

To obtain some answers I had to again refer to the Holy Scriptures. (Good News Bible) Matthew 5:2-12.

a) Happy are those who know they are spiritually poor...

b) Happy are those who mourn...

c) Happy are those who are humble...

d) Happy are those whose greatest desire is to do what God requires...

e) Happy are those who are merciful to others...

f) Happy are the pure in heart...

g) Happy are those who work for peace...

h) Happy are those who are persecuted because they do what God requires...

i) Happy are you when people insult you and persecute you and tell all kinds of evil lies against you because you are my followers...

The New American Bible uses the words "blessed" instead of "happy," showing that happiness is indeed a blessing.

In studying the several instances of happiness listed in the Holy Scriptures, one can see that they give a clear indication that happiness is definitely not like some clothes where one size fits all, so it necessitates that we look at some a little closer to glean some insight into happiness.

Let us look above at i) "Happy are you when people insult you and persecute you and tell all kinds of evil lies against you because you are my followers."

Does that mean a human being, who like all other human beings, likes people to like, respect and care for them, will be emotionally happy when people insult, persecute them and tell evil lies about them that they know to be untrue? They certainly will not be ecstatic and joyful in their mind and body but within them in the place called soul and spirit they will be happy.

Again, when a human being is humble as in c) above, thinking of others more highly than himself, gets trampled on, passed over for promotion, never praised for doing a good job while other people who did nothing get the praise, when this humble person sees that is he happy? Certainly not in his mind and body, but again in his soul and spirit he is happy.

In the case of h) above, a human being is doing what God wants of him, to love his enemy who persecutes, terrorises rejects him and causes others to do the same to him as he sees his home blown up or faeces thrown through his letter box or bricks through his window or his wife or husband and family insulted, is he happy? Most certainly not in his mind and body but in his soul and spirit he is, because he knows that his reward is great.

I use these examples to show that it is very possible to be happy and sad or disappointed at the same time in the same body because man is made up of a body, (senses, brain, arms and legs etc) Soul (inner self where "gut Feelings" and "vibes" or creative ability abides) and Spirit which governs the body and soul.

It is therefore possible to have conflicting emotions but the spirit may be embedded with happiness or unhappiness; this is why a person can be enjoying the good life and propelled by the embedded unhappiness in his soul would go on to self-harm.

At the same time a person can be in atrocious conditions but the happiness in his spirit causes him to be patient and endure.

A person can experience a "good life" while embedded in unhappiness in his spirit. It would make the "good life" meaningless to that person so there is obviously more to being happy than "the good life."

Generally there needs to be a synchronisation of body, soul and spirit to enable the good life to give happiness. Take, for an example, if only one man is enjoying the good life could he rest in contentment while all those around him are starving?

CHAPTER FIVE
SELF-WORTH

In the previous chapter we discussed the "good life" with its deceptions and shortcomings.

Is it possible that one's assessment of one's self-worth could be an underlying link to happiness?

Could the self-worth rating of oneself operate independently of other people's perceptions?

Does self-worth always have to be affirmed?

Examples:

a) A young man believes he is good at football, he practises and plays well, however, in conversation with his peers no one tells him he is good, so even though he knows to himself he is better than most others, his own mannerisms and behaviour indicate a lack of confidence.

Suddenly peers and acquaintances confirm that he is very good and at once his mannerisms start to change, he plays with confidence and performs better.

Sadly, though, the cousin of brilliance, arrogance, generally starts to show as well and would need to be contained.

b) A boxer believes he is good but in the ring he gets knocked out frequently. His self confidence becomes low and he then thinks he is not good enough to be a champ.
Suddenly fans affirm him, he behaves like a winner and he starts to win, thus becoming a champion.

There is a saying that no man is an island, which turns out to be true as man appears to need man to achieve great heights in anything, and that need remains even when one has achieved enough to enjoy "the good life," therefore enforcing the point that man by himself alone cannot fully enjoy the "good Life " as it could prove to be a very lonely life.

It would therefore appear that happiness is a mix of many things including sharing of whatever one has achieved with others and being affirmed as in the case of Angelina Jolie.

"She spoke about her experiences with drugs and depression, and recalled the time, in 1997, when she almost hired a hitman to kill her, as well as the three days, just before her marriage to <u>Billy Bob Thornton</u>, that she was sectioned at <u>UCLA's</u> psychiatric ward.[17] By the mid-2000s, Jolie's involvement with the <u>UNHCR</u> and the adoption of her son Maddox had transformed her public image from Hollywood eccentric into humanitarian and devoted mother.[111][147]"

She now appears to be happy and contented by having a large family made up of six children which, no doubt, she would give up even fame or the "good life" for.

If, therefore, the good life as we were programmed to believe to be the "thing" that one should work for is not all it was purported to be, then what is?

If what we have been striving after is vanity, then what is to be the purpose of striving for success if the very measure of success is flawed?

Is there more to it, then, and what therefore is that missing element which could be so serious as to cause "successful" people to end their lives due to emptiness of life, even when they are the envy of ordinary folk who model their lives on such successful people?

Let us examine Angelina Jolie as mentioned earlier despite fame was envious of the characters she portrayed who seemed to have a more exciting life than her but now with a large family and a man she loves who loves her she is contented and enjoying a life where her family is the purpose of her life transformed to the point where she is also a goodwill ambassador striving to spread goodness of life to others less fortunate.

This shows clearly that without a sense of purpose in this busy striving after success life even to the point of success and beyond it does not seem to make sense.

It appears that man is made to be communal. Sharing of one's life, sharing of success, sharing of ideas, if not part of one's life could result in a feeling of utter loneliness even in company, a craving that seems to be unable to be satisfied without intervention of friends, counsellors or spiritual [advisers?].

It is held in some circles that a re-orientation of the heart is required in order to allow a new appreciation of one's "successful position" and further allows for one to "see" the plight of others. Joanna Lumley, who took on the plight of the famous fighting Gurkas in obtaining British citizenship status, is an example of note.

Another example is Bill Gates of Microsoft fame, who is using his massive wealth to fight diseases worldwide and in Africa in particular.

How can this re-orientation of a heart which was fashioned to go after what is tangible be transformed to "see" the intangible things around him relevant to happiness?

To do this on one's own is nigh impossible as what he needs cannot be bought, or seen and is in fact outside of human realm and would need one to tap into an all powerful source mightier than any ordinarily encountered to bring this change about.

There is, however, a way. The Bible tells us it is in a person who is the son of the Almighty God whose name is Jesus, because that Almighty God made provision for this when He said in JN 3:16 "God so loved the world that He gave his only Son that whoever believes in Him may not die but may have eternal life." Therefore whoever, meaning every human being regardless of his past social standing, education race or creed who believes in God's only son Jesus, and what He did for the salvation of souls, can re-orient his heart to the point where he can "see" things that were not possible before and by so doing would bring happiness and peace to his heart preparing it for being able to enjoy the "REAL GOOD LIFE" through and in Jesus Christ.

Surrendering one's old way of thinking to God's only son Jesus, defined as the way, the truth and the life and accepting Him henceforth as one's saviour, a simple prayer like **"Lord Jesus I need you into my life, I am sorry for the wrong things that I have done, I surrender totally to you henceforth, come into my life."** This would allow Jesus to come into your life and by the presence of supernatural power, "the Holy Spirit" over time would completely re-orient your way of thinking and would then make real living possible with the real possibility of that good life continuing even beyond life on earth. For we know that it is given to men once to die, therefore all men shall die at the appointed time or even before by one's own doing.

CHAPTER SIX

The concept of death has intrigued and fascinated man for thousands of years.

The Egyptians in times past believed it was a passage to another world, we know now, however, thousands of years later, that what they expected did not take place because the treasures which were stored in their tombs were discovered still in the tombs where they were first placed and obviously did not move across with the dead person who incidentally did not pass into the other world physically as even their mummified bodies were still present when discovered.

It was clear even then that life on earth ends at death, but it has been held by some learned men that maybe some form of life continues after.

Is death, however, the end or is there more? This is something to think about seriously but while young it seems something to address later in life and when older it seems too close and too morose.

The Babylonians believed life on earth ends in death.

The ancient Ethiopians, thousands of years ago, believed that life on earth ends at death.

The Hindus believe that life on earth ends at death.

The Moslems believe that life on earth ends at death.

Talking of death, the term could also apply to dying to a way of life such as dying to oneself where although the body is craving for certain things the person denies themselves of that which is craved for until the body gives up the craving and maybe even craves for new things.

Atheists believe that life on earth ends at death.

Christians believe that it is appointed for all men once to die and it further says in the Book of Psalms (Ps) 146 at verse (Vs) 4 "on that day his plans perish," meaning the plans of the one who dies. It is very clear to man that life on earth, as we know it, ends at death.

What is not clear, however, is whether it is actually the final state of man and since mortal man has not crossed back after death except Jesus, we have no documented facts although there has been records of near death experiences which have been verified. We will explore some of these later in the book.

Some beliefs hold that there is re-incarnation, though not necessarily as another person nor in the same place on earth and it is often heard said in conversation "that in a former life I was etc."

We will explore, further, about what happens after one dies, later in this book but suffice for now that life on Earth irrefutably ends with death.

Scientists have had problems even with defining death. At what point is one actually dead, whatever that point is, man universally accepts that, it is a fact, all must die. So regardless of the exact moment it is still agreed that all men once will die.

Is death a passage? Is it a final end? Is it a point of departure? Or is it a moment of receiving rewards for a good or bad life on earth when one is released from the restrictions of a physical frame which deteriorates with age?

These questions could easily occupy one's mind for a lifetime but since we do not have this amount of time, we have to accept that man generally will die once.

I use "generally" because there are some instances recorded in Holy Scriptures, one such being in the book of 2 Kings 2:11, "as they walked on conversing a flaming chariot and flaming horses came between them and Elijah went up to heaven in a whirlwind," (The New American version) he did not actually die but was taken up alive into heaven hinting also that there is a place called heaven after death.

Another was Enoch given in Genesis 5:24, "then Enoch walked with God, and he was no longer here, for God took him," (New American Version) this also indicating that he did not die before being taken by God.

There are a few more listed in the Bible but entering into discussion on this topic would take us outside of the scope of this book.

We can now take for granted that all men will die ending all physical activities on earth, then the person is buried or cremated, and then what?

CHAPTER SEVEN
AND THEN COMES THE
JUDGEMENT

WHAT IS JUDGEMENT?

Judgement is an assessment of a series of actions such as at the end of a trial when the judge gives his judgement or ruling.

This can also take place in several ways:

i) One overeats for several years, more than is needed, with a consequence of obesity with the judgement being a series of health problems which, if despite this, the overeating continues the person's life becomes unbearable leading even to early death.

Judgement could therefore be administered by situations, by persons, or counter reactions but will surely come at or towards the end of a lifestyle followed during the period called life.

ii) If the life is one of moral abuse the judgement could be administered by associates, courts, authorities, institutions or even the Supreme authority.

Is there any way of avoiding this judgement for a life lived wrongly or of even obtaining the judgement for a good life?

The saying goes, IT IS GIVEN ONCE TO DIE THEN COMES THE JUDGEMENT.

Judgement could be seen as a reward for life lived on earth, bad for bad and good for good.

In our discussions we have already looked into the deception of "the good life" and discussed the re-orientation of the heart to make the good life become the real good life, this can be done at any stage of living with the result that once done sincerely with the new fruits of obedience to God's will it changes judgement into reward while alive and when the journey ends at death.

I do not believe that our maker intended us to live a life fearing a judgement at the end but wants us to live rightly in His sight daily so that He can fulfil what His son said, " I have come that you may not only have life but life abundantly," in an envelope of protection and many blessings throughout.

However, at the end of this life on Earth will come a judgement.

CHAPTER EIGHT
WHAT HAPPENS AFTER DEATH?

As no one except Jesus has died and been raised up from death, one can only get an insight from inspired writing.

A Jew named Shalaliel, also called Ezra and Esdras, a learned scribe, prayed and fasted for several weeks and was told in a vision by a messenger of God most high what happens upon death.

The following was taken as is from the second book of Esdras which is found in "the Good News Bible."

Please note that the "I" mentioned therein is Esdras.

[75] 'I answered and said, "If I have found favour in thy sight, O Lord, show this also to thy servant: whether after death, as soon as every one of us yields up his soul, we shall be kept in rest until those times come when thou wilt renew the creation, or whether we shall be tormented at once?"'

[76] 'He answered me and said, "I will show you that also, but do not be associated with those who have shown scorn, nor number yourself among those who are tormented."'

From this one can see that there are two options after death those who will be tormented and those who will not.

[78] Now, concerning death, the teaching is: When the decisive decree has gone forth from the Most High that a man shall die, as the spirit leaves the body to return again to him who gave it, first of all it adores the glory of the Most High.

[79] And if it is one of those who have shown scorn and have not kept the way of the Most High, and who have despised his law, and who have hated those who fear God --

[80] such spirits shall not enter into habitations, but shall immediately wander about in torments, ever grieving and sad, in seven ways.

[81] The first way, because they have scorned the law of the Most High.

[82] The second way, because they cannot now make a good repentance that they may live.

[83] The third way, they shall see the reward laid up for those who have trusted the covenants of the Most High.

[84] The fourth way, they shall consider the torment laid up for themselves in the last days.

[85] The fifth way, they shall see how the habitations of the others are guarded by angels in profound quiet.

[86] The sixth way, they shall see how some of them will pass over into torments.

[87] The seventh way, which is worse than all the ways that have been mentioned, because they

shall utterly waste away in confusion and be consumed with shame, and shall wither with fear at seeing the glory of the Most High before whom they sinned while they were alive, and before whom they are to be judged in the last times.

This therefore is what will happen to the ungodly or unsaved who spent their lives doing ungodly things even while experiencing the "good life."

THE FATE OF THOSE WHO FOLLOWED THE MOST HIGH EVEN THOSE WHO EXPERIENCED THE GOOD AND ABUNDANT LIFE:

[88] "Now this is the order of those who have kept the ways of the Most High, when they shall be separated from their mortal body.

[89] During the time that they lived in it, they laboriously served the Most High, and withstood danger every hour, that they might keep the law of the Lawgiver perfectly.

[90]Therefore this is the teaching concerning them:

[91] First of all, they shall see with great joy the glory of him who receives them, for they shall have rest in seven orders.

[92] The first order, because they have striven with great effort to overcome the evil thought which was formed with them, that it might not lead them astray from life into death.

[93] The second order, because they see the perplexity in which the souls of the ungodly wander, and the punishment that awaits them.

[94] The third order, they see the witness which he who formed them bears concerning them, that while they were alive they kept the law which was given them in trust.

[95] The fourth order, they understand the rest which they now enjoy, being gathered into their chambers and guarded by angels in profound quiet, and the glory which awaits them in the last days.

[96] The fifth order, they rejoice that they have now escaped what is corruptible, and shall inherit what is to come; and besides they see the straits and toil from which they have been delivered, and the spacious liberty which they are to receive and enjoy in immortality.

[97] The sixth order, when it is shown to them how their face is to shine like the sun, and how they are to be made like the light of the stars, being incorruptible from then on.

[98] The seventh order, which is greater than all that have been mentioned, because they shall rejoice with boldness, and shall be confident without confusion, and shall be glad without fear, for they hasten to behold the face of him whom they served in life and from whom they are to receive their reward when glorified.

[99] This is the order of the souls of the righteous, as henceforth is announced; and the aforesaid are the ways of torment which those who would not give heed shall suffer hereafter."

[**100**] I answered and said, "Will time therefore be given to the souls, after they have been separated from the bodies, to see what you have described to me?"

[**101**] He said to me, "They shall have freedom for seven days, so that during these seven days they may see the things of which you have been told, and afterwards they shall be gathered in their habitations."

[**102**] I answered and said, "If I have found favour in thy sight, show further to me, thy servant, whether on the day of judgment the righteous will be able to intercede for the ungodly or to entreat the Most High for them,

[**103**] fathers for sons or sons for parents, brothers for brothers, relatives for their kinsmen, or friends for those who are most dear."

[**104**] He answered me and said,......." I will show you this also. The day of judgment is decisive and displays to all the seal of truth. Just as now a father does not send his son, or a son his father, or a master his servant, or a friend his dearest friend, to be ill or sleep or eat or be healed in his stead,

[**105**] so no one shall ever pray for another on that day, neither shall any one lay a burden on another; for then every one shall bear his own righteousness and unrighteousness."

[**42(112)**] He answered me and said, "This present world is not the end; the full glory does not abide in it; therefore those who were strong prayed for the weak.

[**43(113)**] But the day of judgment will be the end of this age and the beginning of the immortal age to come, in which corruption has passed away,

[**44(114)**] sinful indulgence has come to an end, unbelief has been cut off, and righteousness has increased and truth has appeared.

[**45(115)**] Therefore no one will then be able to have mercy on him who has been condemned in the judgment, or to harm him who is victorious."

CHAPTER NINE
OUT-OF-BODY EXPERIENCES

We know of only one person who died and rose from dead (Jesus), but there are many recorded experiences of people who have died for short periods who recovered and their experiences give us an insight of what one can expect during the seven days mentioned by Esdras above:

As one researches, there seems to be a common thread: they all saw themselves separated from their bodies and was able to view clearly what was going on. Some experienced travelling by thought waves at great speeds, passing through physical objects like walls, some were able to identify objects while out of the body which turned out to be correctly located after. They were able to see loved ones and would talk to them but they the loved ones could not hear.

I have linked to this website for further reading for any interested in knowing more:
http://near-death.com/experiences/research11.html

I have taken a couple examples to make the point.

The NDE and Out-of-Body

Kevin Williams' Research Conclusions

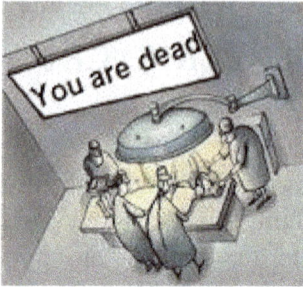

Imagine that you are a patient in a hospital and surgery is being performed on you. You are sound asleep. You were sound asleep long before they wheeled into the operating room. But while you are asleep something very strange happens. During the operation, you are suddenly awakened to find yourself floating near the ceiling! Down below are the doctors working on your body (as in the cartoon on the left). You see a strange sign hanging from the ceiling which says "you are dead." You watch as the doctor puts the electric paddles on your chest. You have a wonderful peaceful feeling which you have never had before. The doctors give your body a shock and you are back in your body sound asleep again. Hours later, you awaken and tell the doctor about your out-of-body experience and the "you are dead" sign. The doctor smiles and tells you, "Your heart stopped during surgery and we had to revive you. You are part of a near-death study and you had a near-death experience. You are the first patient who has ever read that sign. That sign can only be read by someone reading it from the vantage point of the ceiling. And because you were able to read this sign and tell us about it, you have proven scientifically that the mind can function outside of the body. A great scientific discovery has just occurred. Congratulations. This is probably how researchers are going to prove scientifically that our consciousness can transcend our bodies."

Example ii.

Seven hundred cases
A most highly credible scientist, Dr Robert Crookall, analyzed over seven hundred reports of OBEs. He found that 81% of those who had experienced them had a firm conviction of life after death owing to their personal experience. What astounded Crookall, a meticulous scientist, was the consistency of the reports of OBEs coming from all over the world with near death experiences and with the communications coming from high level mediums (Crookall 1970).
This is used to indicate that there have been many cases of out of body experiences. This shows clearly that another form of existence exists especially after death.

Example iii.
Lewis J Experience
1/5/13 "As I floated higher, embraced by the warm air and the beautiful angel singing, my spirit, (that very part of us that our Father placed there when we were ourselves created) began to awaken. It was like someone had turned the ignition on, I was getting closer and closer to the top of the precipice, my eyes which were closed could see the light becoming even brighter, the warm air became

increasingly absorbing my anxiety was gone, this place felt like home. Love. I sensed that not so far away from where I was going there was waiting a very special person, the brilliant warm white light appeared to radiate from a circular area not so far away and from it came the most overpowering and enveloping feeling of pure Love. I was almost leaping for joy, I knew in that very same instance that it was Jesus who was there, even though I didn't see him his loving presence was quite prevalent. My spirit and very being was filled to overflowing with pure love, much stronger than any humanly ties, I knew instinctively that I was loved eternally and was astonished to know that my Lord could ever contain so much "Love" just for me. In that very same moment, I found myself sitting up in bed, out of breath in a state of shock/surprise, where had I been? This wasn't just a dream, it was a journey that I'd been sent on."

It seems clear that it is given to men once to die and then comes the judgement; it is definitely not the end but a separation from an earthly existence in a body that restricts to another existence where thought governs movement and communication does not use speech but some kind of telepathy. The quality of that "afterlife" will definitely be determined by how the period from birth to death is used here on earth.

Well respected psychiatrist Elizabeth Kuber Ross has researched extensively on the afterlife and has written books on the matter. In an online excerpt taken from one of her books

She said: "Since I have worked with terminally ill patients for the last two decades, I have become more and more preoccupied with looking at the phenomena of death itself. We have learned a lot about the process of dying but we still have many questions with regard to the moment of death and to the experience our patients have at the moment they are pronounced medically dead.

It is research such as Dr Moody presents in his book which will enlighten many and will confirm what we have been taught for two thousand years—that there is life after death."

For further reading for those seeking more information:

http://www.amazon.co.uk/Life-After-Elizabeth-Kubler-Ross/dp/0712602739/ref=pd_sim_b_2#reader_0712602739.

This book has been written to try to correct some of the ideas we were given as children which fashioned our later years causing much distress and confusion and resulting in many hardships and discomforts.

It also strives to show that is not too late, while here on Earth, to make a far-reaching change which could cause us to enjoy "the good life" here on Earth and after death to continue it into eternity.

I know there are some other concepts of what happens after death, however since I believe that

Jesus is the truth, I did not consider that there was any worthwhile purpose in looking at those others.

In conclusion:

A child is born. The primary responsibility lies first with the parents to nurture, love, care and form this child in preparation for future life. During that time one has to be extremely careful not to "pass" one's fear, biases, likes and dislikes to the new mind as later on in life these can be very difficult to correct.

Formation exposes the child to further learning where positive or negative influences can take their toll on the new mind. By that time the child's character starts showing up and good can be reinforced and bad corrected.

High school takes place with further learning, and then comes the commencement of life.

Striving after success begins equipped only with ideas and motivations obtained to date.

How we live, interact, balance, fun, enjoyment of things achieved and reflection comes in on what is next, what is life all about, how does one accumulate wealth, what to do with and about it.

How can one ensure a full life, and then what happens at death and what happens after death?

We started with more questions than answers but by now we should have many more answers. However, answers only lead to more questions.

I sincerely hope that this book has opened minds to what is important and what is not.

EPILOGUE

On reading this book the question may come to the mind of the reader, asking what is the objective of the book? Where is it going?

Very good questions, so I will try to explain the reason for the book.

I myself have been a victim to the same things, my mother brought me up to the best of her ability, bless her, in very trying circumstances. I survived, was formed and got the best education that I could at that time, succeeded to be a Fellow Member of the Institute of Engineering and Technology (F.I.E.T), worked as a senior project engineer in a telecoms firm as a design engineer.

I discovered along the way those things mentioned in the book, so I decided to write this book in a bid to cause one to pause along the way, look at his or herself and the world he or she lives in to make any adjustments early. That would enable the person to achieve the very good life in balance and doing the things necessary that he (meaning he or she as explained in the introduction) could go on to have a good life here on earth and thereafter when having died once.

In keeping with the words of Jesus written in John, "I came not only to bring life but life abundantly."

John 10:10b, "I am come that they might have life, and that they might have it more abundantly."[2] "More abundantly" means to have a superabundance of a thing.

"Abundant life" refers to life in its abounding fullness of joy and strength for mind, body, and soul.[3] "Abundant life" signifies a contrast to feelings of lack, emptiness, and dissatisfaction, and such feelings may motivate a person to seek for the meaning of life and a change in their life.[4]

Abundant life teachings, that God is a good God who wants to bless people spiritually, physically, and economically.

May the Lord Jesus bless everyone who reads this book and strengthen those who are already in Him and give the grace to the others to be open to accept Him as Lord.

Ron Abraham

www.ingramcontent.com/pod-product-compliance
Lightning Source LLC
Chambersburg PA
CBHW051433090426
42737CB00014B/2961